Good Dog!

Kids Teach Kids About Dog Behavior and Training

Evelyn Pang and Hilary Louie

Dogwise Publishing

Wenatchee, Washington

Good Dog! Kids Teach Kids About Dog Behavior and Training.
Evelyn Pang and Hilary Louie

Dogwise Publishing
A Division of Direct Book Service, Inc.
403 S. Mission St. Wenatchee, Washington 98801
1-509-663-9115, 1-800-776-2665
www.dogwisepublishing.com / info@dogwisepublishing.com
© 2008 Evelyn Pang and Hilary Louie

Illustrations: Evelyn Pang
Graphic Design: Lindsay Peternell

Library of Congress Cataloging-in-Publication Data
   Pang, Evelyn, 1993-
   Good dog! : kids teach kids about dog behavior and training / Evelyn Pang and Hilary Louie.
   p. cm.
   ISBN 978-1-929242-58-0
   1. Dogs--Behavior--Juvenile literature. 2. Dogs--Training--Juvenile literature. I. Louie, Hilary, 1993- II. Title.
   SF433.P356 2008
   636.7'0887--dc22
   2008028489

ISBN13: 978-1-929242-58-0
Printed in the U.S.A.

Contents

More praise for Good Dog!

Congratulations to Hilary Louie and Evelyn Pang! With mentorship from Lynn Loar, they have created a marvelous resource on communicating safely and effectively with dogs that I will make available to both children and adults.

Barbara W. Boat, Ph.D., Associate Professor, University of Cincinnati Department of Psychiatry; Director, The Childhood Trust, Cincinnnati Childrens' Hospital Medical Center

Good Dog! Kids Teach Kids About Dog Behavior and Training is a wonderful addition to the dog training literature and unique in that the authors are children. Hilary and Evelyn clearly explain the powerful clicker training method and include humor, empathy and information kids need to understand what their canine friend is thinking and how to keep themselves safe around dogs.

Joan Orr, M.Sc., President, Doggone Safe www.doggonesafe.com

Good Dog! Kids Teach Kids About Dog Behavior and Training is a very informative and endearing book. You and your children will have a wonderful time learning how to teach and interact with dogs.

Jesús Rosales-Ruiz, Ph.D., Associate Professor, Department of Behavior Analysis, University of North Texas

This unique approach to training dogs reflects a deep compassion for both animals and children. Through the eyes of the two child-writers, this book focuses on responsible care, safe interaction, and effective communication with dogs. Yet, from it, the astute reader can glean much about the minds and hearts of children as well.

Cheryl Joseph, Ph.D., Professor, Animals in Human Society Program, Department of Sociology, Notre Dame de Namur University

Acknowledgments

The material in Chapters 1 and 2 is adapted for children from Joan Orr's web sites, www. doggonecrazy.com and www.doggonesafe.com, and Turid Rugaas's book *On Talking Terms with Dogs: Calming Signals,* with Ms. Orr's and Ms. Rugaas's permission.

The information in Chapter 3 is adapted for children from Karen Pryor's *Clicker Training for Dogs* with Ms. Pryor's permission. A shorter version was first published in *Teaching Empathy: Animal-Assisted Therapy Programs for Children and Families Exposed to Violence* by Lynn Loar and Libby Colman, published by the Latham Foundation in 2004. It is also available in English, Spanish, and Chinese as a brochure at these web sites: www.thepryorfoundation.org and www.doggonesafe.com. A version of the brochure accompanies the DVD *Clicker Puppy* by Joan Orr available through www.doggonesafe. com.

The Strategic Humane Interventions Program (SHIP) designed by Lynn Loar, through which the authors learned clicker training, was supported by the San Francisco Department of Animal Care and Control, the Humane Society of Sonoma County and a grant from the California Governor's Office of Criminal Justice Planning (OCJP).

The authors are delighted to thank the many people who helped and encouraged them to write this book. Joan Orr, Barbara Boat, Karen Pryor, Jesus Rosales-Ruiz, Kay Laurence, Turid Rugaas, and Lisa Clifton-Bumpass made many helpful suggestions as this book took shape. Ayumi Meegan took the photos of the authors that accompany their biographies and critiqued the manuscript. David Gordon gave invaluable advice about printing and publication. Mary Tebault meticulously proofread the final manuscript.

A Note for Parents and Dog Trainers

What a pleasure it is to introduce you to dog behavior and training through this clear and witty book written and illustrated by and for children! The authors, now middle school students of considerable experience both as shapers of behavior and as writers, began their careers by participating in a dog training program offered in the community room of their apartment building in the Tenderloin section of San Francisco. With dogs from the city shelter, Evelyn, Hilary, and a number of their friends and neighbors learned how to teach dogs good manners and useful skills—sitting, coming when called, waiting rather than grabbing food, etc.—that would make the dogs more adoptable and easier to live with.

Evelyn and Hilary wanted to do extra work and decided to write a book about what they had learned. There's lots of information available about training dogs, but it's all written by adults for an adult audience. There's also lots of material on safety around dogs, written by adults for children. But, there's really nothing written by and for kids—that is, until now.

Good Dog! Kids Teach Kids About Dog Behavior and Training tells parents and children what they need to know to understand their dog, play safely with their dog, and teach their dog all sorts of tricks and useful behaviors. It gives practical examples and terrific illustrations that teach people of all ages how to deal with dogs, annoying younger brothers and sisters, and teachers—even those who call on you when you don't know the answer.

So, get ready for a great read! As the girls say, you'll have the best time getting to know and training your dog!

Lynn Loar, Ph.D
President, Pryor Foundation

Introduction

You Can Have a Good Dog Too!

We used to be afraid of dogs and didn't know much about them. While learning clicker training and writing this book, we've grown to respect and appreciate dogs and care about them. We know that dogs are like humans—they like food, like to play, like to be loved, and DON'T like to be yelled at or punished. Dogs can't speak our language, so they use their body to express their feelings. When you understand dogs through their movements, you will know how they feel and what they want. You won't be afraid of getting bitten.

We wrote this book so people can be safer around dogs and enjoy them as much as we do. This book won't get you mad. It won't get you sad. It will only make you glad. You'll have the best time getting to know and training your dog!

In Chapter One, you'll learn about your dog's movements and feelings.

In Chapter Two, you'll learn how to be safe when you play with your dog.

In Chapter Three, you'll learn how to have fun training your dog.

There are questions at the end of each chapter so you and your parents can test yourselves. There's a glossary at the end with big words that you can use to impress your parents and teachers.

This book is fun and entertaining, and you won't only learn about your dog—you'll also learn about everyday life. Have a great time reading our book. We hope you enjoy it!

Chapter 1

What is Your Dog Trying to Tell You?

Dogs can tell you their feelings, what they need, and their attitudes by the way they move and the way they look. Sometimes, dogs' movements are really hard to see—but they are easy to figure out once you know what to look for. In this chapter, we'll tell you what to look for so you'll know your dog's language and attitude.

Looking at Your Dog's Body

Dogs come in many different breeds and mixes of breeds. Some are tiny and some are almost as big as a pony. Some have ears that stand up and some have ears that hang down. Their tails are different too. They can be short, long, or in-between; straight, curly, or hardly there at all! In order to know how a dog is feeling and what he* is thinking, you have to know what he usually looks like.

*We didn't want to use "it" because a dog is a living being, not an object. We use "he" in this book because it can get confusing to say "he" sometimes and "she" at other times. We mean both male and female dogs.

To understand what your dog is feeling and thinking, here are some things to look for. Look at your dog's eyes, mouth, nose, tail, ears, and fur. Look at all parts of the dog's body, not just one. As you get to know your dog, you will see which movements your dog chooses to show you how he feels.

After you finish reading about your dog's movements in this chapter, you'll begin to notice that other dogs use this language too. You may also notice that some of their movements are different than your dog's, but you will still know what they are trying to tell you and other dogs.

Can you tell if this is a happy or a sad dog?

Eyes

Where a dog is looking is a way of telling you how he is feeling and what he is thinking about.

If your dog is happy, he will look at you but not stare. If your dog is scared or wants to be left alone, he will look away from you. If your dog is angry, he may stare straight at you. Half moon eyes (the white part of the eyes looks like a half moon) mean your dog is really, really angry and may be about to bite you.

HAPPY

These dogs are looking at you, but not staring.

you can see that the eyes make a half moon ☾.

When the whites of the eyes form a half moon, watch out!

Tail

The tail is an important part of a dog's body that he uses to let you know what he is thinking about and how he is feeling. A tail will tell you if your dog is happy, angry, scared, or wants to be left alone. Like a person's smile, or wide eyes, a dog's tail shows feelings and attitudes.

If your dog is happy, his tail will wag in a relaxed way. How it wags depends on the length of his tail. If your dog's tail is short, it will wag in little circles. If it's long, it will make bigger circles, semi-circles, and side-to-side wags. A few dogs, Great Danes and Greyhounds especially, keep their tails low. So when they are happy, they may wag their tails lower than other dogs.

If your dog is scared or wants to be left alone, he puts his tail between his legs, pointed toward his belly. If your dog's tail is short, it will go down and towards the belly as far as it can go.

If your dog is angry, he will have his tail up and wagging stiffly.

Be careful if you see a dog with a stiff tail pointing up. A happy dog will have a more relaxed tail.

Ears

Some dogs have ears that stick up and other dogs have ears that hang down. Because dogs' ears are so different, you have to know how your dog moves his ears when happy, sad and angry.

Usually a dog who is wagging his tail and has his ears up is happy. A dog who is standing or sitting stiffly with his mouth closed and ears forward probably wants to be left alone. A dog whose ears are back and close to his head is angry, scared, or worried and should be left alone.

Look at other parts of your dog's body before deciding what your dog's ears are telling you.

EARS FRONT

These dogs are pointing their ears forward and their tails are stiff. They are probably not happy.

Mouth

If your dog is happy, his tongue may be out. Some dogs look like they are smiling, but some don't. Their lips will be relaxed.

If your dog is scared or wants to be left alone, he may lick his lips when there's no food around, lick his paw, or yawn when he is not tired. If your dog is angry, he might growl, show his teeth, or shut his mouth really tightly. Your dog might bark to show anger.

Your dog may pretend to bite you by putting his mouth on your arm or leg, but not bite down. If your dog mouths you without biting down on purpose, he is giving you a warning. This is called **bite inhibition** 🐾 (words and terms you may not know are shown in bold followed by a paw print and are defined in the glossary at the end of the book). If you ignore the warning, then your dog won't pretend anymore.

This dog has a relaxed mouth and looks happy.

Nose

Dogs can smell more things than humans can. They can smell where you have been and what you have had to eat recently. Dogs can learn a lot just by sniffing you. Sometimes they sniff you to see if they want to be mean or nice to you. After they have smelled that you are not dangerous, they'll be more relaxed.

Your dog smells you to find out more about you. Dogs do the same thing with other dogs. If the other dog welcomes the attention, your dog will smell the other dog's face and bottom. Most of the time when dogs meet each other, they run around in circles to sniff each other.

If your dog is scared or wants to be left alone, your dog may not sniff you or another dog. Instead, he might choose to smell something else, for example, a bush, some grass, or the ground. This kind of sniffing usually means your dog is uncomfortable. People have to learn what this behavior means, but other dogs almost always know what it means and will stay away until your dog begins to relax. If your dog is really anxious or angry, he may start sniffing a long way away from you or another dog. Your dog may growl or bark at the same time.

If your dog is scared or wants to be left alone,
he may sniff the ground to avoid you.

Fur

A dog's body is covered with fur. Some dogs have short fur and some have long fur. It is easy to see fur move on short-haired dogs, but harder to see on long-haired dogs. By watching how a dog's fur moves on his body you can tell how he's feeling. If you can't see the hair going up because your dog's fur is long, pay extra attention to other things your dog is doing so you don't misunderstand how your dog is feeling.

If your dog is happy, the fur is how it normally is. If your dog is excited, scared, or angry and wants to be left alone, the fur on his hackles (between the shoulders) and the spine (all the way to the tail) rises.

Hackles Up

This dog's hackles are up because he is excited,
scared, or angry and wants to be left alone.

Looking at Your Dog's Movements

Animals who live in groups learn how to communicate or "talk" with each other so they will be able to hunt together, have babies, make friends, and live with each other peacefully. Having arguments is dangerous, because fights cause injuries. They have to get along with each other to protect themselves from enemies. If they didn't, they would probably die out.

Humans have to learn dogs' language to be friends. This section will teach you how dogs talk so that people and dogs can talk to each other.

What are Calming Signals?

Calming signals 🐾 are body movements that people and animals who live in groups use to keep situations from becoming dangerous. Calming signals show others that you're not angry or trying to hurt them and that you want to avoid danger. Turid Rugaas explains all about these signals in her book *On Talking Terms with Dogs: Calming Signals* and her web page www.TuridRugaas.com.

You use calming signals every day but you may not know it. For example, if you're trying not to get called on by the teacher you may grab a tissue or drop something and duck down to get it. You can also drink water or pretend you're coughing—make sure to keep coughing until the teacher calls on another person!

Here is a calming signal you might have tried: "Maybe If I look busy the teacher will not call on me!"

Dogs use calming signals also, but humans don't usually understand them. For example, if you want your dog to come to you, you should not yell "COME!" If you do yell, then your dog may get scared and walk slowly to you. You might think your dog is not listening to you so you yell louder. Your dog will get more scared and walk even more slowly or walk away. Then, you might get angry because you think your dog isn't respecting you. Don't misunderstand your dog. Calm yourself down. When your dog slows down, he's asking you to calm down because you are scaring him.

Here are Some Calming Signals

Walking Slowly

When you want your dog to come and he responds by walking slowly, it means, "You are scaring me." In order to make your dog feel safer, try to use a calm and relaxed voice.

Looking Away

Sometimes dogs look away from humans and other dogs because they are trying to get out of danger. Dogs look away to get out of fights. Dogs and puppies understand that looking away means, "I don't want any trouble." Looking away is a useful calming signal because it prevents fights and reduces danger. Humans often misunderstand the meaning of looking away. Humans think looking away means you're not respecting them. When humans feel disrespected, they get angry. The more they get angry, the more the dog gets scared and looks away (because you don't want to look at the angry face, do you?).

If your dog looks away from you, he is scared and may want to be left alone.

These dogs are trying to stay relaxed by not looking directly at each other.

Turning Away/Turning the Head Away

Dogs turn their heads away to tell you or other dogs that they don't want to cause trouble.

Sometimes people do the same thing. For example, if you see angry people around you, you may look away from them. If you look straight at them, it often means you want to cause trouble. With friends or people you know, don't turn your head away when they are looking at you because they might think you're being disrespectful to them.

Curving

Walking in a curve is a bigger version of looking or turning away. Walking in a curve is using your whole body instead of just using your head to say, "Let's not fight." For example, if you are walking in the street and you see someone who makes you uncomfortable, you would want to walk in a big curve around that person so you won't get into a fight.

Sometimes humans misunderstand when dogs curve away. They think it is a way of disrespecting them and they get angry. When the person gets angry, the dog gets scared and makes a much bigger curve. The dog makes a curve because he wants to avoid anger.

If you are walking your dog on a leash and your dog starts to curve, he wants to avoid whatever he's curving away from. It's a good idea to let your dog curve as far away as he wants from whatever is scaring him.

These two dogs are staying calm by curving away from each other.

Freezing

Freezing is when a dog stops or becomes very still because he's not sure if the person, animal, or thing in front of him is dangerous or safe. Dogs freeze in different positions like lying down, sitting, and standing.

When you look angry, your dog may freeze to tell you to calm down. Or, instead of just freezing, your dog may walk slowly and then freeze, walk slowly and freeze. Freezing is a serious warning that your dog is angry or frightened and may be about to bite.

Play Bow

When your dog's hind legs are up, his front legs are down on his elbows, and he is looking up at you, your dog is doing a play bow. Play bow has two meanings. One meaning is that he is asking you or another dog to play. The other meaning is that he is feeling scared and is doing a play bow to show that he isn't dangerous. This is a calming signal that helps make a dangerous situation less dangerous.

If your dog does a play bow, it means either that your dog wants to play or that he is trying to make the situation less dangerous by using a calming signal. You have to look at your dog's surroundings to see which meaning the play bow has.

Sniffing the Ground

Sniffing is a dog's special ability. Sometimes dogs use their special ability to tell us that they're scared. When people or dogs walk by them, they may sniff the ground if they think the people or dogs are dangerous. Dogs also sniff the ground when they see or smell new things. You have to look at your dog's surroundings to see if something might be scaring him or if there is something really smelly on the ground that interests him.

Sniffing the ground is sometimes a calming signal.

Licking the Lip

Licking the lip is a way dogs show people and other dogs that they don't want to cause any trouble. Licking the lip is a calming signal that dogs use often. No matter how big or small the lick is, other dogs will always see it.

Licking the lip is different from panting. Panting is when a dog's tongue is sticking out and the dog's breathing is loud and fast. Panting usually means the dog is really hot or very stressed. You can tell the difference because when the dog licks, his mouth is not wide open and his breathing is not loud. The dog only licks once or twice. With panting, the tongue is hanging out and the mouth is wide open. Dogs pant until they cool down or calm down.

If your dog licks his lip, he is using a calming signal that means he doesn't want to cause trouble. (If your dog is panting, give him some water and a cool place to rest.)

Yawning

When a dog yawns, it doesn't always mean the dog is tired or bored. Sometimes it means the dog is scared and is trying to say "stop."

If your dog yawns when he's not tired, he wants you, or other people or animals, to stop doing the thing that is scaring him.

Urinating (peeing)

Urinating is a calming signal like yawning, but it is a bigger calming signal that dogs use when really scared.

If your dog urinates (pees) because he is scared, stop scaring him and don't get mad. If you get mad, you will scare your dog even more and he will continue to urinate.

Conclusion

Now that you understand dogs' movements, you'll know what your dog is trying to tell you. You can use your understanding of these calming signals to make your dog feel relaxed around you. The next chapter will teach you to be safe around dogs.

Test Yourself

1. What do dogs' movements tell you?

2. How do dogs' movements help them survive peacefully?

3. When do dogs and people use calming signals?

4. How do calming signals keep you safe? How do calming signals keep dogs safe?

5. Give three examples of calming signals that your dog uses.

Congratulations! You are a person who can understand your dog's movements and communication—but don't get too excited because you have more to learn in the next chapter.

Chapter 2

Be Safe When You Play With Your Dog

Do you and your friends want to play safely with your dog? Do you want to learn how to prevent dog bites? In this chapter you'll learn how to be safe around dogs.

Your dog is a lot like you in many ways, even if you don't always know what your dog is thinking. You wouldn't want a stranger to come over and hug and kiss you—so you should not do that to a dog you don't know. Your friends may be strangers to your dog so you should warn them not to do that. Although you are not a stranger to your dog, he might not like it if you hug and kiss him. Even if your dog usually doesn't mind, he may if he is not in a good mood, is tired, sick, or injured. Your dog may use calming signals like looking away to tell you that he doesn't want to be hugged or kissed. If you or your friends ignore the calming signals, your dog might snap or bite.

You don't want a stranger to go near your food while you're eating, or near your toys and other belongings, so don't go close to dogs when they are eating or playing with their toys and belongings. You also wouldn't want a stranger to wake you up while you are sleeping, so don't wake a dog when he is sleeping. Respect dogs like you would human beings. Be extra careful when your dog is eating, playing with a special toy, or sleeping.

Dogs put up with many annoying human behaviors from their owners, but not from strangers. This means you should be especially careful around other people's dogs and make sure your friends are especially careful around your dog.

How to Be Safe Around Dogs

- If a dog is sleeping, do not pet him.

- If a dog is eating or drinking, do not bother him. The dog might think you're trying to steal his food.

- If a dog has any other belongings, especially things he really likes, don't try to take them. The dog might think you're stealing them. Dogs want to keep their belongings. They guard them. This is called **resource guarding**. ❀ Resource guarding is like a girl protecting her diary and other important things she doesn't want to be stolen (this is really important if you have a little brother or little sister!). Dogs are like people with diaries. The diary is the resource and the dog is guarding it. Leave dogs alone when they're playing with their resources.

- If you run around a dog or chase a dog, or when kids play tag around a dog, it may not be safe because running excites dogs. They may chase and even try to bite as part of the game of chase. For kids' safety, do not let them play tag or run around your dog.

WHAT MAKES IT UNSAFE AROUND DOGS?

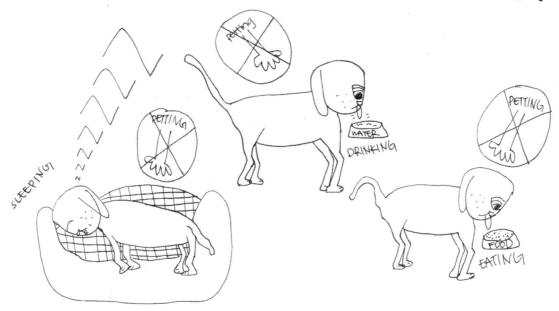

Be careful around a dog when he is doing these things!

How Can You Tell a Dog May Be About to Bite?

- When the dog bares (shows) his teeth.

- When the dog gives you a mean stare.

- When the dog has half moon eyes.

- When the dog freezes.

- When the dog growls.

- When the dog is leaning forward on tippy toe, stiff, and tense.

- When the dog's tail is stiff. It can be up or down; it may wag stiffly and slowly.

- When the fur on the dog's hackles (back) goes up.

- When you wake a sleeping dog—the saying "let sleeping dogs lie" means never wake up a sleeping dog because he'll be surprised and might bite you.

- When you are near a dog who is eating, drinking, or guarding resources. The dog might glare or growl at you, or eat or drink faster.

- When a child is annoying or bothering the dog. The dog may turn his head away, walk away, glare, or growl.

- When a child is running or screaming around the dog.

- When the dog chases or tries to catch the child.

How Can You Prevent Bites from Happening?

- Ask your parent or babysitter first for permission to play with any dog.

- Ask the owner to have the dog sit so you can pet him safely. If the dog sits, then go ahead. If the dog doesn't sit, do not pet him. It may not be safe.

- Ignore dogs who are tied up outside or in a fenced yard.

- Ignore dogs inside parked cars. If the owner is away and the car windows are open, don't stick your hand in the parked car to pet the dog.

- If a dog is friendly, the dog will welcome you with tail wagging and other happy signals. If he does not welcome you, leave the dog alone. If you're not sure, leave the dog alone.

- Ask your parent or babysitter and the dog's owner if you may pet somebody else's dog—never pet strange dogs whose owners are not around. Only ask the owner if the dog is awake and seems interested in attention.

Always ask if you may pet a dog.

Always stay away from a dog tied up outside.

How to Go Up to a Dog Safely

Walk slowly toward the dog with your face sideways so you don't stare at the dog. Staring at the dog's face may make the dog think that you want a fight.

How to Stand Near a Dog

Don't lean or step over the dog. Sit down to welcome small dogs or dogs who are lying down. To most dogs, kids seem big—even if they look small to other kids. Sitting down makes you seem smaller and less scary to the dog.

How to Extend Your Hand to a Dog

Dogs greet animals and people by sniffing. So, put your relaxed hand out for the dog to sniff. Do this before you touch the dog.

Let the dog sniff your hand before petting him.

How to Touch a Dog

Sit beside the dog. Gently scratch the dog's chest or side in the direction of the fur. Pat the dog on the shoulder closer to you. Use long, gentle strokes in the direction of the fur. Don't reach across the dog, put your face close to the dog's face or lie on the dog. Don't hit or poke the dog, or pull the dog's ears, tail, or fur.

Think about when you are busy doing something and don't want to be annoyed—so you ignore your younger brother. He starts poking you or doing something very annoying until you pay attention. This is how your dog feels when you poke or pull his ears, tail, or fur.

After petting the dog, move your hand away slowly. Dogs chase after fast moving things—including people's hands.

How to Give Treats to a Dog

Drop the food on the ground and let the dog get it or hold the treat in a flat open hand a little lower than the dog's head so the dog can lick it from your hand. If you hold the food too high or move your hand around, the dog will jump to get the food.

How to Play Safely With a Dog

Chapter 3 teaches you a great new way to train your dog called **clicker training** that lets you play all kinds of games with your dog. You can also play hide and seek and fetch. Don't play tug of war or chasing games with the dog. Don't dress up the dog.

How to Go Away From a Dog

Walk away slowly. Jumping or running away will excite the dog. The dog may think you are starting a game of chase.

Playing tug with a dog is sometimes OK for an adult, but not for a kid.

What to Do if a Dog Runs Up to You

Be Safe When Standing or Moving

If a strange or scary dog comes near you, or even if your own dog is getting too frisky, stop moving and stand very still. Keep your arms still and look down at your feet. This will let the dog know that you want to be left alone.

Doggone Safe (www.doggonesafe.com), a great program that teaches children how to be safe around dogs and how to avoid dog bites, says to "Be a Tree: stop, fold your branches, and watch your roots grow."

Stop: Stand very still; don't move even an inch.

Fold your Branches: put your arms down, your hands together and keep them very still.

Watch your roots grow: Look at your feet.

Try to be the most boring person in the world by standing very still so the dog will lose interest in you.

Be Safe When Sitting or if You Fall Down

Curl up like a ball, put your hands on your neck and cover your neck and head with your arms. Try to be the world's most boring person.

Pretend you are in an earthquake drill. You cover your head with your hands and arms to protect yourself from falling objects.

Always stand very still when a strange or scary dog comes near you.

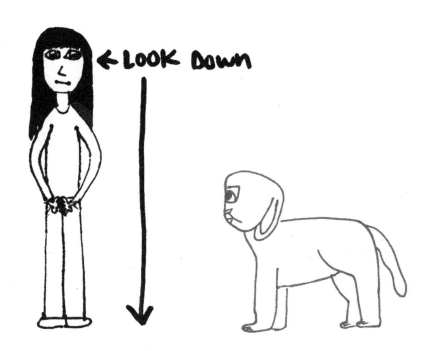

←LOOK DOWN

Test Yourself

1. What is it called when you protect your stuff?

2. Why do you think dogs get upset when you go near their belongings?

3. You see a dog tied to a pole. What should you do?

4. What should you do before you pet a dog who does not know you?

5. What should you do when a scary dog runs up to you? What if you fall down?

Congratulations! You are a person who can protect yourself—but don't get too excited because you have more to learn in the next chapter.

Chapter 3

The BEST Time You'll Ever Have Training Your Dog!

Teaching Good Manners and Tricks with a Clicker and Treats

Is your dog like mine was? Does he jump and bark when friends come to the door? Does he run away or pull on the leash?

Would you like your dog to learn good manners and even tricks?

Teaching your dog good manners and tricks can be really easy with a clicker and treats. Once you know that teaching your dog tricks is easy, you can make up your own tricks.

If you want to find out how much fun it can be to teach your dog good manners and new tricks, read on!

What is Clicker Training?

Clicker training 🐾 is a game you play with dogs and other animals—even people—to teach good behaviors. All you need is a **clicker** 🐾, this information, and some **treats.** 🐾 If you learn what is in this chapter, you'll be able to train your pet yourself. You'll learn how to make learning fun. And you'll learn ways to say "yes" to your dog by clicking and giving treats for good behaviors while ignoring bad ones.

What is a Clicker?

A clicker is something that makes a short, sharp sound. You can buy clickers at pet supply stores and at www.clickertraining.com. Local animal shelters and dog training programs may also have clickers for sale.

If you don't have a clicker, or if your dog is afraid of the loud sound some clickers make, use a retractable pen (a pen with a button on top that you push to make the point come out) or a Snapple® bottle cap which also makes a soft clicking noise.

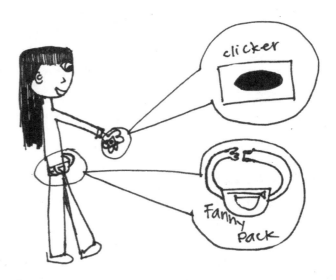

You will need a clicker like this and a fanny pack for treats.

What Treats to Use

When you begin training a dog, you should always have a parent or other adult with you to make sure the dog is safe around food. Some dogs are not used to working for their food. They may try to nip or bite you to get the food. Let your parents give the dog the first few treats to make sure the dog doesn't nip or bite while being given the treat. If the dog barks, growls, or tries to grab the food, give all the food to the dog and stop the training session. This means you and your parents need a professional trainer.

If your parents have decided it is safe for you to give treats to the dog, use treats that the dog really, really likes. Most dogs like cheese, hot dogs, and chicken. You can also use treats made especially for dogs—something better than regular dog food—if you don't want to use human food. Chop the treats into tiny little pieces so you and the dog can play the training game for a long time before the dog gets full.

How to Click

Hold the clicker with your thumb on the part that makes the short, sharp sound.

Click when you think the dog's behavior begins to get close to what you want. So if you are teaching a dog to sit, click when he sits or if he tries to sit and comes close. Give a treat right after you click.

The trainer must always look at the dog and pay attention to the dog. If the trainer looks away when the dog sits, the dog will be frustrated because he didn't get the click and treat he earned. He may not want to do it again. If you make it fun, easy, and interesting, the dog will want to do it.

Never hurt or **punish** 🐾 the dog. Don't pull the dog's leash. Never use force. Find a way the dog will like to do the behavior.

How to Treat

Put the treats somewhere you can reach easily and fast like your pocket or a fanny pack. You can also put the treats in a bowl easy for you to reach, but away from the dog. Give the dog a treat by dropping it on the ground in front of him or holding the treat in your open hand.

Drop the food on the ground   or   hold the treat in a flat open hand

If you take a long time to get the treat and give it to the dog, the dog may think that he won't get a treat after that click. He may not understand that he did something right. He may get confused, lose interest, and not want to pay attention anymore.

The trainer must give a treat with every click. The dog may think, "If I don't get a treat when I hear the click, I won't do it again." The trainer has to respect the rule that the treat must follow the click right away. The treat has to be something the dog really likes.

Click once and give extra treats when the dog is close to the movement. Don't click more than once—let the extra treats show that you like the behavior a lot.

What to Click For

Pick something easy at first. Click and treat for an easy task and then make it a bit harder. This is called raising **criteria**. When you start, click and treat for a step in the right direction. Remember, the dog's a beginner! Go step by step. **Increment** is a big word for step. Click and treat for each step (increment) so the dog takes incremental steps toward the goal. For example, if you want your dog to come to you, click and treat when the dog looks at you, takes a step toward you, takes two or three steps toward you, and click and give lots of treats when the dog comes all the way.

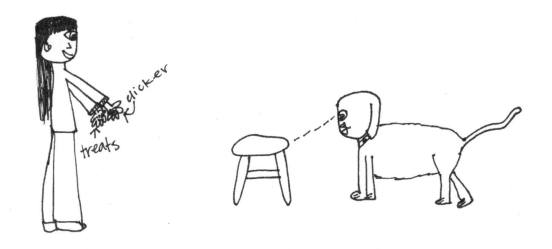

If you want to train your dog to sit on a stool, click
when he looks at or moves towards the stool.

Click and treat for something the dog is already doing. The click tells the dog, "You're close to the movement." Click and treat for accidental moves toward the goal. Click and treat for what you want—no yelling, no complaining. Ignore mistakes.

Don't give orders. If the dog doesn't respond to you, he is not being bad. He just doesn't understand what you want him to do. Make it easier. Go step by step, with very small steps. Then make the steps bigger.

Pay attention. Don't get distracted. When the dog is trying, be nice, give more time, and extra treats. Don't be bossy. You will seem mean and the dog will think he is bad. Rely on the power of clicker training.

Click and treat good or useful behaviors whenever you see them. When your dog does something cute or useful, click and treat. It may be surprising for the dog at first. The behavior will get better and better if you click and treat often.

When to Click (Timing ❀)

Click when the behavior happens, not after.

Click a lot and click often when the dog is being taught a behavior for the first time. Otherwise the dog might get confused or disappointed and not want to do it again.

If it's not going well, you're probably clicking late. If you click late, you're not paying close attention to small steps.

Don't wait too long to click. Don't wait for the whole behavior to click. Click for something close to the movement. For example, if you want the dog to jump over a hurdle, first click when the dog looks at, points at, or takes a step toward the hurdle. Then, click for getting closer to the hurdle.

How to Make the Behavior Better

When the dog gets the idea of what you want, then expect a bit more for each click. The dog starts to know the behavior you want. The dog does the behavior better. This is called **shaping the behavior.** 🐾 Shaping the behavior means making it better step by step.

When the dog can do the basic behavior, click and treat only for the better tries. For example, if your dog knows how to sit, begin to click and treat only for the better sits. This means that you may click and treat the first sit, then the third or fourth, then the sixth, and so on. How often you click and treat is called the **rate of reinforcement.** 🐾 Changing the rate of reinforcement makes the behavior better and makes the session more exciting because the dog doesn't know what's going to happen next. Clicking less often and only for the better tries is called **intermittent reinforcement.** 🐾

Now that your dog is pretty good at the behavior, begin to make it harder by teaching your dog to do the behavior in many places. When your dog can do the behavior anywhere, teach your dog to pay attention to the behavior even if other things are going on nearby. Introduce **distractions,** 🐾 things that may take the dog's attention away from the task, one by one.

For example, smells are important to dogs and make it hard for dogs to pay attention to the task. Dogs also like to chase things that move. They distract the dog and make it hard for the dog to concentrate. So, at first teach indoors, in a quiet place. Then introduce one distraction (like going outdoors) and see if the dog can concentrate. If the dog can concentrate, try another distraction. If the dog is having trouble concentrating, go back to the quiet place and practice. Reminder—it's not the trainer getting distracted—it's the dog! Consider what would distract the dog, not you.

Use **jackpots** 🐾 (a large handful of treats given all at once to the dog) when the dog gets the behavior or makes a lot of progress all of a sudden.

How to Succeed With the Clicker

Keep practice sessions short. Five minutes once or twice a day is plenty. Short sessions help dogs (and other learners) concentrate. They learn more with a few short tries. Breaks help. Dogs remember easily with short sessions and breaks.

Try training another behavior if you can't get what you are after. If you get mad—stop. Don't force yourself. Don't yell at the dog. Take a break and do it later.

Remember, make it fun!

Jackpot!

Clicker Do and Don't Lists

Do:

- Click on time
- Click for every good behavior
- Give a treat for every click
- Click often for beginners
- Look at the dog
- Pay attention at all times
- Ignore distractions
- Give a handful of treats (a jackpot) if the dog is close or gets it right
- Help by clicking a lot when teaching a new behavior
- Help by clicking a lot if the dog gets frustrated
- Pick something easy for beginners and something harder for intermediate and advanced dogs
- Make sure it's safe

Don't:

- Look away from the dog
- Click more than once for the same correct behavior
- Forget to click
- Forget to treat
- Walk away, get impatient, or show disrespect in other ways
- Get distracted
- Click for no reason
- Click late
- Frustrate the dog by not paying attention to him
- Punish the dog

Here are Some Tricks You can Teach Your Dog with a Clicker and Treats:

Teaching Your Dog to Sit

1. Show your dog the treat by putting it in front of his nose.

2. Bring the treat up and back a few inches from the dog's nose to the top of the dog's head. The dog's nose will follow the treat. The dog's nose will go up and the tail will go down. This is called **luring** ❧ the dog into a sit.

   Keep the treat close to the dog's head. If you lift the treat too high, the dog will jump. The dog might sit all the way or just a little. If the dog sits a little bit, click and treat. If the dog sits all the way, click and give the dog a jackpot.

3. Do that a few times so the dog can remember it.

4. When the dog has the idea, you won't have to bring the treat all the way from the dog's nose to the back of his head. You can begin to shrink your hand movement and the dog will still understand that he should sit. With practice, you can shrink your hand movement a lot so you'll barely need to move your hand. This is called **fading the lure.** ❧

5. Then, make it a little harder. Have the dog sit longer. Then click and give the dog a treat.

Click and give your dog a treat when he sits.

Cueing Your Dog to Sit

1. Teach the behavior using a clicker and treats (see above) and make sure your dog sits almost every time.

2. Say "sit" as the dog begins to sit. The word "sit" is the **cue** 🐾 for the dog to do the behavior. Click when the dog sits and treat. You can use another word or hand signal instead of "sit" if you want. Do that a few more times and the dog will remember the cue and the movement.

3. Now say "sit" before the dog sits. If the dog sits, the dog knows the word. Try putting away the clicker and telling the dog to sit. If the dog doesn't sit when you say "sit," the dog doesn't know the word "sit" yet. Do numbers 1 and 2 again. If the dog sits, say "OK" and give the dog a treat. Do this a few more times so the dog learns that "OK" means, "You don't have to do the behavior any more." "OK" is a **release word** 🐾, something that tells the dog he can stop doing the behavior. When the dog knows the cue and the release word, you don't need to click or treat that behavior every time. Click and treat "sit" once in a while so the dog stays interested in the behavior.

Teaching Your Dog to Lie Down

1. Cue the dog to sit.

2. Get a treat and put it in front of the dog's nose. Lower the treat to the ground. The dog's nose will follow the treat down. You are luring the dog down. Move the treat straight down. If you move it away from the dog's body, the dog will get up to follow it.

3. If the dog goes lower, click and treat. You may have to do this a few times for the dog's body to go all the way down.

4. Do that a few times so the dog can remember it. Always click and treat when he does it right.

5. When the dog has the idea, begin to fade the lure.

6. Then, make it a little harder. Have the dog stay down a little longer. Then click and give him a treat.

Click and treat as your dog gets lower and lower.

...n a clicker and treats (see page 62).

...c dog begins to go down. The word "down" is the
...ﾁ to do the behavior. You can use another word or hand
...stead of "down" if you want. Do that a few more times and
...dog will remember the cue and the movement.

3. Now say "down" when the dog is sitting. If the dog goes down, the dog knows the word. Try putting away the clicker and telling the dog "down." If the dog doesn't go down when you say "down," the dog doesn't know the word "down" yet. Do numbers 1 and 2 again. If the dog lies down, say the release word "OK" and give the dog a treat. When the dog knows the cue "down" and the release word, you don't need to click or treat that behavior every time. Click and treat "down" once in a while so the dog stays interested in the behavior.

Teaching Your Dog to Target 🐾 Your Hand

Hand targeting is when the dog taps your open hand with his nose. You teach hand targeting because you can help your dog to walk near you, to go where you want, and to do tricks like spinning around, rolling over, and crawling under chairs and tables by following your open hand.

1. Put your hand out near the dog's nose. The dog may sniff your hand. If the dog taps your hand with his nose, click exactly when the dog's nose touches your hand and treat. The dog may only move toward your hand at first. Click and treat that.

   If the dog ignores your hand, rub a little cheese or other treat on your hand so the dog can smell it and try again. If the dog taps or licks your hand, click during the behavior and treat. You may have to do this a few times for the dog to understand. Then try without rubbing the treat on your hand.

2. Put your hand farther back so the dog has to move more to tap it with his nose. If the dog targets your hand, click and treat. If the dog does not target your hand, try again, but make it a bit easier for the dog by putting your hand closer.

3. Then, move your hand under or over something so the dog learns to follow your hand. Repeat until the dog understands and follows your hand. Remember to click and treat often when the dog does it correctly.

4. To help shape the dog's behavior, click for the better tries (intermittent reinforcement).

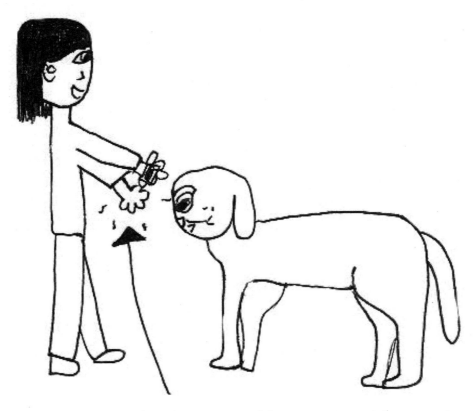

A good way to get your dog interested in your hand is to rub food on it!

Cueing Your Dog to Target Your Hand

1. Teach the behavior with a clicker and treats (see above).

2. Say "touch" when the dog's nose begins to touch your hand. The word "touch" is the cue for the dog to do the behavior. You can use another word or hand signal instead of "touch" if you want. Do that a few more times and the dog will remember the cue and the movement.

3. Now say "touch" just before the dog's nose touches your hand. If the dog targets your hand, the dog knows the word. Try putting away the clicker and telling the dog "touch." If the dog doesn't target your hand when you say "touch," the dog doesn't know the word "touch" yet. Do numbers 1 and 2 again. If the dog targets your hand, say the release word "OK" and give the dog a treat. When the dog knows the cue "touch" and the release word, you don't need to click or treat that behavior every time. Click and treat "touch" once in a while so the dog stays interested in the behavior.

Using Hand Targeting to Teach Coming When Called

Make sure the dog knows the word "touch." Try stretching your arm out so the dog has to go farther to target. As you practice, go farther and farther away for the hand target. When the dog has the idea, say "come" (when you would have said "touch"). That way your dog will know two cues for this behavior.

Using Hand Targeting to Teach Walking on a Leash Without Pulling

Put a leash on your dog. Put your hand out and say "touch" while you are walking. The dog stays near you to keep touching your hand. Click and treat a few times for a step near you, then for three steps. If the dog does that, go longer. Make it more advanced. Click and treat for a different number of steps near you. This is another example of using intermittent reinforcement. If the dog doesn't stay near you, go back and click and treat every step. Try again to make it more advanced. Keep doing that and the dog will get used to it and walk close to you.

Targeting a Stick

A **target stick** is a narrow stick about 2-3 feet long that has tape, a small ball, or another marker at its bottom. This is the target. You can make a target stick, or you can buy one at www.clickertraining.com or your local pet supply store.

target with a stick

fanny pack with treats

You hold the plain end of the stick in your hand and teach the dog to tap the other end (the tape, ball, or other marker) of the stick with his nose so you:

- Don't have to bend or reach down
- Can work farther away from the dog
- Can teach the dog not to pull on the leash
- Can teach the dog to go to different places, under and over objects
- Can teach the dog to turn in a circle
- Can teach the dog tricks

Teaching Your Dog to Target a Stick

1. Hold the plain end of the target stick in your hand and put the other end of the stick near the dog's nose. The dog may sniff the stick. If the dog touches the stick with his nose, click exactly when the dog's nose touches the stick and treat. The dog may only move toward the stick at first. Click and treat that. Next, click and treat for touching the stick anywhere. Then, click and treat only for touches closer to the target part of the stick. With a little practice, your dog will learn only to touch the target and not the rest of the stick.

   If the dog ignores the stick at first, rub a little cheese or other treat on the end of the stick so the dog can smell it and try again. You may have to do this a few times for the dog to understand. Then try without rubbing the treat on the stick.

If the dog bites the stick, use a metal spoon, spatula, or rod. Dogs don't like to bite metal.

2. Put the stick farther back so the dog has to move more to touch the stick with his nose. If the dog targets the stick, click and treat. If the dog does not target the stick, try again but make it a bit easier for the dog by putting the stick closer to the dog.

3. Then, move the end of the stick under or over something so the dog learns to follow the stick. Repeat until the dog understands and follows the stick.

4. To help shape the dog's behavior, click for the better tries (intermittent reinforcement).

Cueing Your Dog to Target the Stick

1. Teach the behavior with a clicker and treats.

2. Say "touch" when the dog's nose begins to touch the stick. The word "touch" is the cue for the dog to do the behavior. Do that a few more times and the dog will remember the cue and the movement.

3. Now say "touch" just before the dog's nose touches the stick. If the dog targets the stick, the dog knows the word. Try putting away the

clicker and telling the dog "touch." If the dog doesn't target the stick when you say "touch," the dog doesn't know the word "touch" yet. The dog may know "touch" for hand targeting, but not for targeting a stick. Do numbers 1 and 2 again. If the dog targets the stick, say the release word "OK" and give the dog a treat. When the dog knows the cue "touch" and the release word, you don't need to click or treat that behavior every time. Click and treat "touch" once in a while so the dog stays interested in the behavior.

Teaching Your Dog Good Manners around Food

If your dog enjoys working for clicks and treats, and your parent thinks it's safe, then it's okay to teach the dog good manners around food.

Food on the Ground

1. Put a treat on the ground and cover it with your hand or your foot. The dog will sniff, lick, and slobber on your hand or foot because he can smell the food.

2. When the dog stops sniffing, licking, and slobbering—even for a second—click and treat.

3. Practice until the dog doesn't sniff, lick, or slobber at all and he doesn't run to the treat. Practice until the dog waits patiently.

Food in Hand

1. Put a treat in your fist. The dog will sniff, lick, and slobber on your hand because he can smell the food.

2. When the dog stops sniffing, licking, and slobbering—even for a second—click and treat.

3. Do this a few more times. Practice until the dog doesn't sniff, lick, or slobber on your hand at all. You want the dog just to look at your hand quietly before you feed him.

Cueing Your Dog to Wait for Food

1. Teach your dog to wait for food with a clicker and treats.

2. Say "off" when the dog backs away from the food on the floor or in your hand. The word "off" is the cue for the dog to do the behavior. Do that a few more times and the dog will remember the cue and the movement.

3. Now say "off" before the dog moves toward the food. If the dog waits, the dog knows the word. Try putting away the clicker and telling the dog "off." If the dog doesn't wait when you say "off," the dog doesn't know the word "off" yet. Do numbers 1 and 2 again.

Test Yourself

1. What don't clicker trainers do when teaching?

2. When you start to teach your dog a new behavior, you:

   a. Wait to click until the dog does the whole behavior.

   b. Click when you want to click.

   c. Click when the dog takes a first step toward the behavior.

   d. None of the above.

3. What does "shaping the behavior" mean?

4. Why should you keep training sessions short?

5. Why should you teach the behavior first and the cue second?

Congratulations! You have become a safe and smart dog trainer, and there are no more "buts" for you. So have fun with dogs.

If you want to learn more about clicker training, go to www.clickertraining.com.

Conclusion

When you started the first page of this book, you probably didn't know that much about dogs. Now you've learned to tell how they feel by their movements. You've learned how to be safe around dogs by using calming signals. And you know how to train dogs with a clicker and treats. You can use all that you have learned to have fun with, befriend, and enjoy your dog.

We told you that you would learn a lot about your dog and how to train him without getting mad or frustrated. So, what do you think about this book? Fun and entertaining, isn't it? You can use clicker training to train your dog, other animals, and people too. With these skills, you can volunteer at an animal shelter.

If you want to learn more about dogs, go to www.doggonesafe.com and www.clickertraining.com.

We hope you enjoyed this book, and remember to click, treat, and have fun!

Glossary

Bite inhibition. The dog may pretend to bite you by putting his mouth on your arm or leg, but not biting down. The dog mouths you without biting down to give you a warning. If you ignore the warning, the dog won't pretend anymore.

Calming signals. A special way to communicate without words used by people and animals who live in groups. Calming signals are used to get away from danger and to show that you're not dangerous.

Clicker. A little device that makes a short and sharp sound.

Clicker training. Training using a clicker to mark good behavior. The trainer clicks when the dog gets the behavior right or gets close to the behavior. The trainer gives a treat to the dog after every click so that the dog will know he got the behavior right and earned a treat for doing the behavior.

Criterion (singular), Criteria (plural). A step or requirement; raising criteria means starting with a step that is very easy and then making it harder and harder.

Cue. A word or hand signal that comes before and asks for the behavior. For example, saying "sit" is the cue for an action.

Distraction. Something that takes your attention away from the task. Don't let the dog get distracted at first. For example, smells are important to dogs and make it hard for dogs to pay attention to the task. Dogs also like to chase things that move. They would distract the dog and make it hard for the dog to concentrate. So, at first teach indoors, in a quiet place. Then introduce one distraction and see if the dog can concentrate. Reminder—it's not the trainer getting distracted, it's the dog! Consider what would distract the dog, not you.

Fading the lure. Making the lure smaller until it disappears, something you do when the dog knows the behavior very well. See **lure.**

Increment. A small step.

Intermittent reinforcement. Clicking and treating less often and only for the better tries (of the same movement). For example, the dog is practicing a jump and the trainer clicks for the higher jumps. This makes the behavior better and makes the session more exciting because the dog doesn't know what's going to happen next. See **reinforcement.**

Jackpot. A large handful of treats that you give the dog when he gets the behavior or makes a lot of progress all at once.

Lure. A treat or something else the dog will want to follow. The trainer holds a treat in his/her hand to get the dog to do a movement by following the treat.

Luring. Getting the dog to follow something to do the behavior. For example, if you put a treat in front of a dog's nose and lift it up and back along the dog's head, the dog's nose will follow the treat. This way you can lure the dog into a sit.

Punish, Punishment. You get punished after you do something wrong. Parents, teachers, coaches, trainers, etc. punish you because you did something wrong or didn't do what they told you to do. You feel mad, sad, ashamed, and that it is unfair. Sometimes you cry. Sometimes you think it is stupid that the person punishes you. Sometimes it affects the relationship between you and the punisher.

Rate of reinforcement. How often the trainer clicks and treats the dog during training.

Reinforcement. A treat or something else that you earn for doing the behavior. Reinforcements make you want to do the behavior again. A dog wants a piece of cheese or meat and a person wants candy. Both learners will repeat behaviors to earn more reinforcers (treats).

Release word. "OK" or some other word (or hand signal) to say to the dog, "You don't have to do the behavior any more."

Resource guarding. Dogs wanting to keep their belongings. Dogs guard them so people and dogs won't take them. Resource guarding is like a girl protecting her diary and other important things she doesn't want to be stolen (this is really important if you have a little brother or little sister, possibly an older brother, but not an older sister because she knows that your diary is really important and it is private). Dogs are like people with diaries. The diary is the resource and the dog is guarding it. Leave dogs alone when they're playing with their resources.

Shaping the behavior. Making the behavior better step by step.

Target. Something you ask the dog to touch for a reward.

Target stick. The dog aims for the end of the stick as his target. The dog taps his nose to the end of the stick. This lets the trainer move the dog around in a circle, under or past things without a leash.

Timing. Clicking at the right time so you reward the right behavior.

Treat. Food or something else the dog enjoys.

Web Sites for More Information

www.aspca.org gives a lot of information about dogs and other animals. It's easy to use. It can help you adopt an animal.

www.clickertraining.com can help you get started and keep on learning about clicker training. You can also find clicker training supplies, videos, and books.

www.dogwise.com sells books about dogs and dog training. The books may reveal different topics that you might enjoy.

www.doggonecrazy.com tells you about the best equipment and supplies for dogs and other animals.

www.doggonesafe.com teaches you many methods to stop dog bites and avoid danger from dogs.

www.hsus.org is good to check out if you want to do research about animals. It has sections on mammals, reptiles, and birds. It also tells you how to protect animals and what to do if you lose your pet.

www.latham.org teaches humane education (teaching people to care about animals).

www.learningaboutdogs.com is about clicker training dogs in England. You might be interested in this site because it is British.

www.nahee.org is well organized and has really cute pictures.

www.thepryorfoundation.org is mainly for adults, but has brochures for children about clicker training in English, Spanish, and Chinese.

www.TuridRugaas.com has detailed information about calming signals. Turid Rugaas wrote a book and made a video about calming signals.

Answers to Test Questions

Chapter 1

1. What do dogs' movements tell you? Dogs' movements tell you their feelings, needs, and attitudes.

2. How do dogs' movements help them survive peacefully? Animals that live in groups have to learn how to talk to each other so they will be able to hunt together, have babies, make friends, and live with each other peacefully.

3. When do dogs and people use calming signals? Dogs and people use calming signals when they are afraid and want to feel safer.

4. How do calming signals keep you safe? How do calming signals keep dogs safe? Calming signals show that you are not dangerous and you don't want to fight.

5. Give three examples of calming signals that your dog uses. Any three of the following calming signals:

- Walking slowly
- Looking away
- Turning away/turning the head away
- Curving
- Freezing
- Play bow
- Sniffing the ground
- Licking the lip
- Yawning
- Urinating (peeing)

Chapter 2

1. What is it called when you protect your stuff? It is called resource guarding.

2. Why do you think dogs get upset when you go near their belongings? Dogs get upset because they think you want to take their belongings.

3. You see a dog tied to a pole. What should you do? You should stay away from the dog.

4. What should you do before you pet a dog who does not know you? Let him sniff your hand first.

5. What should you do when a scary dog runs up to you? What if you fall down? You should freeze and be a tree (fold arms in, look down at your feet). If you fall down, curl up like a ball, put your hands on your neck and cover your neck and head with your arms. Be as boring as possible by not moving and not looking at the dog.

Chapter 3

1. What don't clicker trainers do when teaching? Clicker trainers don't yell, complain, give orders, or make learning hard. They don't get distracted or bossy.

2. When you start to teach your dog a new behavior, you: c. Click when the dog takes a first step toward the behavior.

3. What does "shaping the behavior" mean? Shaping the behavior means making the behavior better step by step.

4. Why should you keep training sessions short? Keeping sessions short helps the dog (or other learner) concentrate easily.

5. Why should you teach the behavior first and the cue second? Dogs have to know the behavior first because they don't understand human language. Once they know the behavior, they memorize the sound and match the sound to the behavior they already know.

About the Authors

Evelyn Pang was born in San Francisco, California in 1993. She attends a Bay Area middle school and goes to a Chinese school every afternoon to study Cantonese and Mandarin. She is fluent in English and Cantonese and enjoys writing Chinese calligraphy. She likes to sing, act, and play sports. She also likes baking cakes and cookies. She loves clicker training and playing with dogs. Evelyn plans to attend high school and college, and hopes to act on the stage.

Hilary Louie was born in San Francisco, California in 1993. She went to China for a few years and came back to the Bay Area to enter kindergarten. She is now in the honors program in middle school. She loves to play the violin and basketball, but not at the same time. Hilary speaks English and Cantonese fluently. She plans to go to high school and, after that, college. Hilary likes clicker training and enjoys dogs. She loves training them, playing with them, and just having fun.